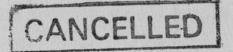

THE AUSTRALIAN
Women's Weekly

CONTENTS

Cocktails and drinks don't have to be complicated – just get the right base, some interesting additons, lots of ice and you won't even need an umbrella! Try making your own garnish with citrus rind or chilli instead. For traditional cocktails with alcohol, mocktails with no alcohol; a glorious fruit smoothie or a juiced combination for that perfect afternoon, these are drinks for all occasions – from Brunch Eye-openers to perfect Nightcaps.

Food Director

Pamela Clark

PERFECT COCKTAILS
TIPS & TRICKS

Whether you're throwing a drinks party or merely mixing a quiet tipple, the following tips will ensure that you're equipped and informed – and the perfect cocktail can be yours.

EQUIPMENT

Behind every good host stands a great blender. You'll need one that is powerful enough to crush ice. You'll also need a cocktail shaker, a strainer, cocktail measuring equipment, a mortar and pestle, swizzle sticks, straws and an assortment of glasses.

GENERAL TIPS

• Since ice is a primary ingredient in many cocktails, it should be handled accordingly. Take it out of the freezer just before using to ensure it is dry. To crush ice, start the blender on low until the ice begins to crush, then switch to high speed. Alternatively, place ice in a clean tea towel or plastic bag and crush with a meat mallet, rolling pin or hammer. If possible, try to use ice that has been freshly made – ice that remains in the freezer, uncovered, can absorb the smells and flavours of other food stored in the freezer.

• The quality of the liquor makes a world of difference. Nothing will mask second-rate alcohol.

• We have specified if fresh juice is required; other-wise, use bottled juice from the supermarket. If a recipe calls for concentrated juice, do not substitute fresh juice, as it is too watery.

• Freeze fresh fruit to make a smoother, less watery drink. For best results, prepare fruit the same day by cutting into chunks, then laying chunks flat in the freezer in a plastic bag. Depending on the variety of fruit, the pieces will be ready in 30 minutes to 1 hour.

BASIC RECIPES

SUGAR SYRUP

Sugar syrup, often called gomme syrup, is used for sweetening drinks.

COMBINE 1 cup (220g) sugar and 1 cup (250ml) water in a small saucepan; stir over low heat until sugar dissolves. Bring to a boil, then reduce heat and simmer, uncovered, without stirring, 5 minutes; remove from heat, cool.
STORE in an airtight container in the refrigerator for up to 2 months.

MAKES about 350ml

SOUR MIX

Sour mix is also known as sweet and sour mix or bar mix.

COMBINE 1 quantity (350ml) sugar syrup (see recipe above), 120ml lemon or lime juice and 1 egg white (this is optional, but will make the drinks slightly foamy).
STORE in an airtight container in the refrigerator for up to 3 days.

MAKES about 470ml

HOT & SOUR MIX

COMBINE 120ml sour mix (see previous recipe) with 4 halved fresh red thai chillies (seeds included).
STIR and refrigerate for up to 3 days. Strain before using.

MAKES about 120ml

MINT SYRUP

FILL a large bowl with ice and water.
BRING a small saucepan of water to a boil. Plunge 2 cups firmly packed fresh mint leaves into boiling water for about 3 seconds. Remove with a slotted spoon, then immediately transfer to iced water until cold; drain.
COMBINE 180ml sugar syrup (see earlier recipe) and mint in a blender jug; blend until pureed, stand syrup for 10 minutes. Push syrup through a fine sieve, pressing down firmly to extract as much liquid from mint as possible, discard mint pulp.
STORE in an airtight container for up to 1 week in the refrigerator.

MAKES about 180ml

TECHNIQUES

SALTING OR SUGARING GLASS RIMS

Rub the flesh of a lime or lemon around the rim of your chosen glass until the whole rim has been evenly moistened with juice. Turn the glass upside down and dip the rim into a saucer filled with salt or caster sugar. Shake away any excess seasoning.

MUDDLING FRUIT FOR 'STICK' DRINKS

A muddler is a thick wooden 'stick'. In this book, we used a mortar and pestle instead; if you own a muddler, though, use it rather than a pestle. To muddle fruit, eg, lime wedges, place lime in tumbler or cocktail shaker then, using muddler, press heavily on lime with a mashing motion. Use crush of fruit and juice, unstrained, in the cocktail.

grapefruit twist

CHOCOLATE CURLS

Spread melted chocolate onto a cold surface (such as marble); when set, drag a sharp knife over the surface of chocolate to make curls. Alternatively, drag a vegetable peeler along the side of a block of chocolate.

GARNISHES

These easy garnishes are a quick way to lend your cocktails the appearance of sophisticated chic.

orange rind knot

chocolate curls

pineapple-leaf spear

TWIST OF CITRUS RIND

Using a small sharp knife or a vegetable peeler in a spiralling motion, peel a long, thin piece of citrus rind from fruit then cut the rind into thin strips. Place the rind in the glass, hooking one end of rind over rim of glass.

KNOT OF CITRUS RIND

Remove strips of rind from fruit using a small sharp knife or a vegetable peeler then cut rind into thin strips. Tie strips into knots – this releases fragrant oil from citrus peel – and drop into drink immediately.

PINEAPPLE-LEAF SPEAR

Using small sharp knife, make a small cut in the bottom-centre of a pineapple leaf. Place cut spear on rim of glass.

CURLED CHILLIES

Using small sharp knife, cut a cross in bottom end of chilli. Place chilli in bowl of iced water; stand for 5 minutes. Place curled chilli on rim of glass.

curled red chillies

CHEERS!

Juices and smoothies prepared in a blender contain a good dose of fibre as the fruit/vegetable pulp is mixed through the drink; drinks prepared in a juice extractor, however, contain only the juice.

Blenders are best suited to soft fruits, such as mangoes, stone fruit, bananas and berries, especially when milk, yogurt or crushed ice is being added. Basically, they are ideal for the preparation of smoothies, lassis and frappés.

Juice extractors are ideal for use with hard fruit and vegetables such as apples, citrus, carrot, celery and other leafy greens. An important consideration when purchasing a blender or juice extractor is how easy it is to keep clean. Any appliance you use for juicing and/or blending should be cleaned immediately, otherwise the fruit pulp can prove very difficult to remove.

DRINKS BY DEFINITION

SMOOTHIE

A smoothie is a combination of fruit and dairy products, such as milk, ice-cream or yogurt, that is blended until thick and smooth.

FRAPPÉ

A frappé is a frozen flavoured liquid (usually a blend of whole fruit – mangoes, pineapple, etc – or fruit juice with crushed ice) that has a slushy consistency.

LASSI

A lassi is an Indian version of a milkshake, except that yogurt is used in place of milk. A variety of spices and fruits can be added to lend their distinctive flavours; other common additives are crushed ice or water. It is often served as a cooling accompaniment to a curry.

BRUNCH EYE-OPENERS

SALTY DOG (V)

1 cup ice cubes
45ml vodka
120ml fresh grapefruit juice

PLACE ice in salt-rimmed (see page 5) glass; add vodka then juice.

GLASS 300ml highball
GARNISH grapefruit rind knot

QUIET SUNDAY (V)

30ml vodka
15ml amaretto
120ml fresh orange juice
½ egg white
ice
grenadine

POUR vodka, amaretto, orange juice, egg white and ice into serving glass. Splash grenadine into glass last.

GLASS 285ml highball
GARNISH orange ring and cherry

SCREWDRIVER (V)

60ml vodka
60ml fresh orange juice
ice

POUR ingredients, one after the other, into serving glass filled with ice.

GLASS 140ml old-fashioned
GARNISH orange slice

salty dog

cajun bloody mary

BLOODY MARY (V)

30ml vodka
salt or celery salt
pepper
dash Tabasco sauce
dash Worcestershire sauce
dash lemon juice
ice
120ml tomato juice

POUR vodka, salt, pepper, Tabasco sauce, Worcestershire sauce and lemon juice over ice in serving glass. Stir with swizzle stick. ADD tomato juice and stir once more with swizzle stick.

GLASS 285ml highball
GARNISH lemon wedge and stick of crisp celery

CAJUN BLOODY MARY (V)

1 cup ice cubes
30ml chilli-infused vodka
10ml fresh lemon juice
dash Worcestershire sauce
dash Tabasco sauce
pinch celery salt
pinch cracked
black pepper
120ml tomato juice

The classic morning-after eye-opener. To make chilli-infused vodka, combine 250ml vodka and 4 fresh red thai chillies in a glass jar, cover; stand for about 5 days or until the vodka is infused with chilli heat. Discard chillies before using.

COMBINE ice, vodka, lemon juice and sauces in glass rimmed (see page 5) with celery salt and pepper; add tomato juice, stir.

GLASS 300ml highball
GARNISH lemon wedge and two straws

RED EYE (Be)

chilled beer
tomato juice

POUR equal quantities of the two ingredients into a chilled beer glass.

GLASS beer glass

FRESCA (V)

1 medium grapefruit,
cut into 8 wedges
1 tablespoon palm sugar
or brown sugar
1 cup ice cubes
45ml vodka
10ml sugar syrup (see page 4)
120ml lemonade

USING a mortar and pestle (or muddler), crush the grapefruit and sugar together.
PLACE ice in glass; add grapefruit mixture and remaining ingredients, stir.

GLASS 300ml highball
GARNISH a straw

HARVEY WALLBANGER (V)

30ml vodka
120ml orange juice
15ml Galliano
ice

POUR ingredients, one after the other, into serving glass filled with ice. Stir with a swizzle stick if desired.

GLASS 285ml highball
GARNISH orange slice and a cherry

sea breeze

SEA BREEZE (V)

In this recipe, you can substitute fresh grapefruit juice for the ruby red grapefruit juice if the ruby red variety is not available.

120ml cranberry juice
30ml ruby red
grapefruit juice
45ml vodka
1 cup ice cubes

COMBINE ingredients
in glass, stir well.

GLASS 300ml highball
GARNISH two straws

passionate affair

PASSIONATE AFFAIR (Ch)

For this cocktail we used canned passionfruit in syrup, which is available from supermarkets.

15ml passionfruit liqueur
10ml passionfruit in syrup
120ml chilled brut champagne

COMBINE passionfruit liqueur and passionfruit in a flute; top with chilled champagne.

GLASS 150ml champagne flute
GARNISH none

MIMOSA (Ch)

10ml orange curaçao
30ml fresh orange juice
chilled champagne

POUR curaçao and juice into glass and top with champagne.

GLASS 140ml champagne flute
GARNISH orange twist

mimosa

scorpion

SCORPION (R)

45ml dark rum
30ml Bacardi
30ml brandy
15ml Cointreau
90ml fresh orange juice
1 cup ice cubes
15ml fresh lime juice

COMBINE rum, Bacardi, brandy, Cointreau, orange juice and half of the ice in a cocktail shaker.
SHAKE vigorously then pour into a glass; add remaining ice and lime juice, stir.

GLASS 300ml highball
GARNISH a straw

MORNING GLORY (Br)

30ml brandy
15ml orange curaçao
15ml pure lemon juice
dash Angostura bitters
dash Pernod
ice

POUR all ingredients into shaker, shake, then strain into serving glass.

GLASS 90ml cocktail glass
GARNISH lemon twist

CORPSE REVIVER (Br)

30ml brandy
15ml Calvados
15ml rosso vermouth
ice

POUR all ingredients into shaker, shake, then strain into serving glass.

GLASS 90ml cocktail glass

TEQUILA SUNRISE (T)

30ml tequila
120ml orange juice
7ml grenadine
ice

POUR tequila and orange juice, one after the other, over ice in serving glass. Drop grenadine through centre of cocktail.

GLASS 285ml highball
GARNISH orange slice and a red cherry

FRUIT COLLINS (G)

For this recipe, you will need to blend about a 10cm-chunk of watermelon then pour it through a sieve to catch the seeds.

1 cup ice cubes
45ml ruby red grapefruit juice
45ml fresh watermelon juice
30ml fresh lime juice
10ml sugar syrup (see page 4)
60ml gin
60ml soda water

PLACE ice in glass; add juices and syrup, one at a time, then gin. Stir, top with soda water; stir again.

GLASS 300ml highball (pictured in background)
GARNISH thin slice of lime and two straws

fruit collins

CITRON CRUSH (N)

½ medium lime, cut into 4 wedges
½ medium lemon, cut into 4 wedges
2 tablespoons palm sugar or brown sugar
4 large fresh mint leaves, torn
1 cup crushed ice
120ml lemonade

USING a mortar and pestle (or muddler), crush lime, lemon, sugar and mint.
PLACE in glass; pour in the fruit mixture, then top with lemonade.

GLASS 180ml old-fashioned
GARNISH a straw

ORANGE, CARROT & GINGER JUICE (N)

1 large orange (300g), peeled, chopped coarsely
1 small carrot (70g), halved lengthways
2cm piece fresh ginger (10g)

PUSH orange, carrot and ginger through juice extractor. Stir to combine.

MAKES 1 cup (250ml)
TIPS Refrigerate all ingredients before making the juice. Serve the juice within 30 minutes of making.

orange, carrot & ginger juice

mango & grapefruit juice

MANGO & GRAPEFRUIT JUICE (N)

½ medium mango (215g), skinned, chopped coarsely
1 small grapefruit (350g), juiced
¼ cup (60ml) water

BLEND ingredients until smooth.

MAKES 1 cup (250ml)
TIPS Refrigerate all ingredients before making the juice. Serve the juice within 30 minutes of making. Alternatively, for a refreshing granita-like snack, freeze the juice until almost frozen then quickly mix with a fork before drinking.

PUSSYFOOT (N)

60ml fresh orange juice
30ml fresh lemon juice
30ml fresh lime juice
dash grenadine
1 egg yolk
ice

POUR all ingredients into shaker, shake, then pour into serving glass.

GLASS 285ml highball
GARNISH orange slice and cherry

TOMATO, CARROT & RED PEPPER JUICE (N)

1 medium red pepper(250g), chopped coarsely
4 medium tomatoes (300g), chopped coarsely
2 medium carrots (240g), chopped coarsely
⅓ cup firmly packed fresh flat-leaf parsley
1 cup (250ml) water
dash Tabasco sauce

BLEND pepper, tomato, carrot, parsley and water, in batches, until pureed; strain through coarse sieve into large jug.
STIR in Tabasco.

MAKES 1 litre (4 cups)
TIPS Refrigerate all ingredients before making the juice. Serve within 30 minutes of making.

FRUIT FANTASY (N)

4 oz fresh orange juice
2 oz pineapple juice
6 strawberries
small slice honeydew melon
small slice cantaloupe
ice

POUR all ingredients into blender, blend until smooth. Pour into serving glass.

GLASS 285ml highball
GARNISH fruit in season

tomato, carrot & red pepper juice

beetroot, carrot & spinach juice

LIQUID LOVE (N)

4 medium frozen strawberries
90ml cranberry juice
10ml sugar syrup (see page 4)
10ml fresh lime juice
1 cup crushed ice

COMBINE ingredients in jug of a blender; blend
on high speed until smooth, pour into glass.

GLASS 150ml cocktail
GARNISH a strawberry and a straw

BEETROOT, CARROT & SPINACH JUICE (N)

1 small beetroot (100g), chopped coarsely
1 small carrot (70g), chopped coarsely
1 cup firmly packed baby spinach leaves (20g)
½ cup (125ml) water

PUSH beetroot, carrot and spinach through juice extractor.
Dilute with the water; stir to combine.

MAKES 1 cup (250ml)
TIPS Refrigerate all ingredients before making the juice.
Serve the juice within 30 minutes of making.

MIXED BERRY SMOOTHIE (N)

250ml frozen low-fat strawberry
yogurt, softened slightly
1⅓ cups (200g) frozen mixed
berries
3 cups (750ml) skimmed milk

BLEND ingredients, in batches, until
smooth. Serve immediately.

MAKES 1 litre (4 cups)

BANANA SMOOTHIE (N)

2 cups (500ml) skimmed milk
2 medium bananas (400g), chopped coarsely
½ cup (140g) low-fat yogurt
1 tablespoon honey
1 tablespoon wheat germ
¼ teaspoon ground cinnamon

BLEND ingredients until smooth.

MAKES 1 litre (4 cups)

banana smoothie

ICED MOCHA (N)

1 tablespoon instant coffee powder
1 tablespoon boiling water
2 tablespoons chocolate-
flavoured topping
1½ cups (375ml) cold milk
4 scoops (500ml) vanilla ice-cream
½ cup (125ml) cream, whipped
1 teaspoon drinking chocolate

COMBINE coffee and the water in large heatproof jug, stir until dissolved.
STIR in chocolate-flavoured topping and milk.
POUR into two large glasses and top each with 2 scoops vanilla ice-cream
and cream, then sprinkle with sifted drinking chocolate; serve immediately.

SERVES 2

SPICED ICED
COFFEE MILKSHAKE (N)

¼ cup (20g) ground espresso coffee
¾ cup (180ml) boiling water
2 cardamom pods, bruised
¼ teaspoon ground cinnamon
1 tablespoon brown sugar
3 scoops (375ml) low-fat vanilla
ice-cream
2½ cups (625ml) skimmed milk

PLACE coffee then the water in coffee plunger; stand 2 minutes before plunging. Pour coffee into small heatproof bowl with cardamom, cinnamon and sugar; stir to dissolve sugar then cool 10 minutes.
STRAIN coffee mixture through fine sieve into blender or processor; process with ice-cream and milk until smooth. Serve immediately.

MAKES 1 litre (4 cups)

MASALA CHAI (N)

For this spicy traditional Indian milk tea, we used English Breakfast tea – but try experimenting with other varieties until you find one that suits your taste.

2 cinnamon sticks
1 teaspoon cardamom pods, bruised
1 teaspoon fennel seeds
½ teaspoon whole cloves
1 teaspoon ground ginger
½ teaspoon ground nutmeg
½ cup firmly packed fresh mint leaves
4 teabags
2 cups (500ml) milk
2 cups (500ml) water
sugar

COMBINE spices, mint and teabags in teapot or heatproof jug. Bring combined milk and water to a boil, pour over spice mixture; stand 10 minutes.
SWEETEN with a little sugar, if desired. Just before serving, strain.

MAKES 1 litre (4 cups)

spiced chocolate milk

SPICED CHOCOLATE MILK (N)

30g dark eating chocolate, melted
2 cups (500ml) milk
1 cinnamon stick

USING a teaspoon, drizzle melted chocolate onto the insides of heatproof glasses.
COMBINE milk and cinnamon stick in medium saucepan, stir over low heat until heated through, but not boiling. Remove cinnamon. Pour milk into glasses.

SERVES 2

masala chai

LAZY LUNCH REFRESHERS

LEMON FRIATTO (V)

30ml citron vodka
30ml limoncello
1 teaspoon finely grated orange rind
1 cup ice cubes
3 medium scoops
lemon sorbet

COMBINE vodka, limoncello, rind and ice cubes in a cocktail shaker; shake vigorously.
PLACE sorbet in chilled glass; pour limoncello mixture over the sorbet.

GLASS 150ml cocktail
GARNISH thin strips of lemon rind and a straw

SPRITZER (Wi)

chilled white wine
chilled soda water

POUR equal quantities of ingredients into serving glass.

GLASS 180ml wine glass

lemon friatto

mint julep

MINT JULEP (Bb)

This cocktail should be made with the best bourbon you can buy.

30ml mint syrup (see page 5)
60ml bourbon
2 cups ice cubes

POUR 10ml of the mint syrup into a chilled glass. Combine bourbon and ice in jug of a blender, blend until smooth.
SPOON bourbon mixture into glass; stir, drizzle with remaining mint syrup.

GLASS 300ml highball
GARNISH a straw

CAMPARI LADY (C)

For a sweeter drink, use bottled ruby red grapefruit juice instead of fresh grapefruit juice.

45ml Campari
30ml gin
120ml fresh grapefruit juice
30ml tonic water
1 cup ice cubes

COMBINE ingredients in a cocktail shaker. Shake vigorously then strain into glass with some of the ice.

GLASS 300ml highball
GARNISH two straws

SADE LEMONADE (W)

1 cup ice cubes
30ml scotch whisky
30ml Midori
50ml bottled apple juice
60ml ginger beer
60ml lemonade

HALF-FILL a glass with ice. Pour remaining ingredients, one after the other, over ice; stir gently.

GLASS 300ml highball
GARNISH a slice of lemon and a straw

RED CORVETTE (L)

We rimmed the cocktail glass with pink sugar; simply add a drop of red food colouring to sugar and mix well.

45ml Frangelico
30ml Midori
4 fresh strawberries
1 cup ice cubes

COMBINE ingredients in jug of a blender; blend on high speed until well combined.
POUR into chilled sugar-rimmed (see page 5) glass.

GLASS 150ml cocktail
GARNISH a straw

COSMOPOLITAN (V)

10ml citron vodka
20ml vodka
30ml Cointreau
60ml cranberry juice
1 lime wedge
1 cup ice

PLACE all ingredients in shaker. Shake, then strain into a chilled martini glass.

GLASS 90-120ml martini
GARNISH twist of lime

cosmopolitan

BELLINI (Ch)

Originally made in Harry's Bar in Venice with prosecco, the region's sparkling wine, a bellini is just as moreish when made with champagne. Use white peaches instead of yellow, if in season.

½ medium peach, peeled, chopped coarsely
chilled champagne

BLEND or process peach until smooth; you need 30ml of peach puree. Spoon into serving glass then top with chilled champagne.

GLASS 140ml champagne flute
GARNISH slice of fresh peach

fruity champagne

FRUITY CHAMPAGNE (Ch)

This drink has its origins in the classic bellini but gains distinction when the grenadine hits the glass. You can peel and puree the peach a short time before you want to serve this cocktail if you mix in the lemon juice to prevent it discolouring.

½ medium peach, peeled, chopped coarsely
5ml fresh lemon juice
dash grenadine
90ml chilled brut champagne

BLEND or process peach until smooth; you need 30ml of peach puree. Combine peach puree in a glass with lemon juice and grenadine; top with chilled champagne.

GLASS 150ml champagne flute
GARNISH a lemon slice

bellini

SANGRIA (Wi)

750ml bottle dry red wine
30ml Cointreau
30ml Bacardi
30ml brandy
½ cup (110g) sugar
2 cinnamon sticks
½ medium orange, peeled,
chopped coarsely
½ medium lemon, peeled,
chopped coarsely
6 medium strawberries,
chopped coarsely
1 cup ice cubes

From humble origins in Spain where it was devised as a long, cool drink to combat the summer heat, sangria has become a popular punch at pubs and parties all over the world. If you want to be authentic, use a dry Spanish wine. This recipe makes about four glasses of sangria.

PLACE ingredients in a large jug; stir until well combined, pour into glasses.

GLASS 250ml highball

MAI TAI (B)

1 cup ice cubes
30ml Bacardi
30ml dark rum
15ml orange curaçao
15ml Amaretto
15ml fresh lemon juice
15ml sugar syrup(see page 4)
15ml fresh orange juice
15ml bottled pineapple juice
10ml grenadine

PLACE ice in glass; pour remaining ingredients, except grenadine, one at a time over ice, stir gently. Carefully add grenadine.

GLASS 300ml pilsener
GARNISH a pineapple slice, a maraschino cherry and a straw

VESUVIUS (T)

30ml tequila	POUR ingredients, one after the other, over ice into serving glass.
120ml orange juice	
15ml Campari	GLASS 285ml highball
ice	GARNISH orange twist

CAIPIROSKA (V)

1 teaspoon palm sugar	PLACE palm sugar and three-quarters of the lime in shaker and
1 lime, cut into eighths	crush with the back of a spoon or end of a rolling pin. Add ice and
½ cup ice	vodka and shake. Pour into a glass with crushed ice. Do not strain.
60ml vodka	
½ cup crushed ice	GLASS 185ml old-fashioned
	GARNISH remaining lime wedges and two short straws

LEFT vesuvius

RIGHT caipiroska

WATERMELON WONDER (N)

120ml cranberry and blackcurrant juice
4 x 5cm pieces watermelon
10ml fresh lemon juice
60ml bottled apple juice

COMBINE ingredients in jug of a blender; blend on
high speed until smooth, pour into chilled glass.

GLASS 300ml highball
GARNISH a straw

WATERMELON &
MINT JUICE (N)

450g watermelon flesh, chopped coarsely
4 mint leaves

BLEND ingredients until smooth.

MAKES 1 cup (250ml)
TIPS Refrigerate all ingredients before making the juice.
Serve the juice within 30 minutes of making.

TROPICAL DELIGHT (N)

*You need about 400g of peeled and chopped pineapple
for this recipe.*

1 small pineapple (800g), peeled, chopped coarsely
4 medium apples (600g), chopped coarsely
2 medium oranges (480g), peeled, chopped coarsely

PUSH fruit through juice extractor. Stir to combine.

MAKES 1 litre (4 cups)
TIPS Refrigerate all ingredients before making the juice.
Serve the juice within 30 minutes of making.

fruity vegetable juice

MINTED TOMATO, LIME & RHUBARB FRAPPÉ (N)

4 cups chopped rhubarb (440g)
¼ cup (55g) sugar
¼ cup (60ml) water
4 medium tomatoes (760g), peeled, deseeded, chopped
2½ tablespoons lime juice
3 cups ice cubes
2 tablespoons chopped fresh mint

COMBINE rhubarb, sugar and the water in medium saucepan; simmer, covered, about 10 minutes or until rhubarb is tender. Let cool.
BLEND or process rhubarb mixture with remaining ingredients until smooth; serve immediately.

MAKES 1.25 litres (5 cups)

FRUITY
VEGETABLE JUICE (N)

2 medium beetroot (600g), trimmed, quartered
3 medium carrots (360g), halved lengthways
3 trimmed celery sticks (225g)
2 small apples (260g), quartered
2 medium oranges (480g), peeled, quartered

PUSH ingredients through juice extractor. Stir to combine.

MAKES 1 litre (4 cups)
TIPS Refrigerate all ingredients before making the juice.
Serve the juice within 30 minutes of making. For a more
tart drink, substitute 1 large grapefruit (500g) for the oranges.

VANILLA
CAFÉ LATTE (N)

⅓ cup (30g) coarsely ground
coffee beans
500ml (2 cups) milk
1 teaspoon vanilla extract

COMBINE ingredients in medium
saucepan, stir, over low heat until
heated through, but not boiling.
POUR through fine strainer into
heatproof serving glasses.

SERVES 2

vanilla café latte

EASY AFTERNOONS

WATERMELON CAIPIROSKA (V)

1 lime, cut into 8 wedges
1 teaspoon sugar
10ml sugar syrup (see page 4)
4 x 5cm pieces watermelon
45ml vodka
15ml Midori
½ cup ice cubes
½ cup crushed ice

USING a mortar and pestle (or muddler), crush 6 lime wedges with sugar, sugar syrup and watermelon.
COMBINE watermelon mixture in a cocktail shaker with vodka, Midori and ice cubes. Shake vigorously then pour into glass with crushed ice; do not strain.

GLASS 180ml old-fashioned
GARNISH with lime wedges, a swizzle stick and a straw

LOVE IN THE AFTERNOON (R)

30ml dark rum
30ml fresh orange juice
30ml cream of coconut
15ml sugar syrup (see page 4)
15ml fresh cream
5 strawberries
ice

POUR all ingredients into blender, blend until smooth, then strain into serving glass.

GLASS 180ml old-fashioned
GARNISH chocolate flake and a strawberry

DEATH IN THE AFTERNOON (P)

22ml Pernod
chilled champagne

POUR Pernod into serving glass. Top with chilled champagne.

GLASS 180ml champagne flute
GARNISH none

watermelon caipiroska

BLOSSOM (B)

45ml Bacardi
15ml fresh orange juice
15ml fresh lemon juice
15ml sugar syrup (see page 4)
ice

POUR all ingredients into shaker, shake, then strain into serving glass.

GLASS martini glass
GARNISH orange and a cherry

MOJITO (B)

4 large, fresh mint leaves, torn
1 tablespoon palm sugar
1 lime, cut into quarters
60ml Bacardi
1 cup ice
soda water

PLACE mint and palm sugar in shaker and crush lightly with the back of a spoon. Add lime, Bacardi and ice and shake.
POUR into a glass (do not strain) and top with cold soda water.

GLASS 285ml highball
GARNISH sprig of mint

sweet martini

SWEET MARTINI (G)

45ml gin
15ml vermouth rosso
1 cup ice cubes

COMBINE ingredients in a cocktail shaker. Shake vigorously then strain into a chilled glass.

GLASS 90ml martini
GARNISH a maraschino cherry

LEFT blossom
RIGHT mojito

redskin

LONG ISLAND ICED TEA (V)

1 cup ice cubes
30ml vodka
30ml tequila
30ml Bacardi
30ml gin
15ml Cointreau
15ml fresh lemon juice
15ml sugar syrup (see page 4)
30ml cola

PLACE ice in glass; add vodka, tequila, Bacardi, gin and Cointreau,
one after the other.
ADD juice and syrup, top with cola; stir.

GLASS 300ml highball
GARNISH twist of lemon rind, mint leaves, swizzle stick and a straw

REDSKIN (V)

Guava juice is available from most supermarkets and delicatessens.

45ml vanilla-infused vodka
30ml strawberry liqueur
120ml bottled guava juice
6 fresh strawberries
1 cup ice cubes

COMBINE ingredients in jug of a blender; blend on high speed until smooth, pour into glass.

GLASS 300ml highball
GARNISH twist of red-apple skin and a straw

TIP To make vanilla-infused vodka, combine 250ml vodka and 2 split vanilla beans in a glass jar, cover; stand for about 5 days or until the vodka is infused with vanilla flavour. Discard vanilla beans before using the vodka.

fallen angel

FALLEN ANGEL (G)

One version of the Fallen Angel cocktail is made with crème de menthe, but this version, using blue curaçao, is more popular with us.

75ml gin
40ml blue curaçao
25ml fresh lemon juice
dash Angostura bitters
1 cup ice cubes
100ml lemonade

COMBINE gin, blue curaçao, juice and bitters in glass; add ice, top with lemonade.

GLASS 350ml piña colada
GARNISH a straw and a swizzle stick

PIÑA COLADA (B)

45ml Bacardi
120ml bottled pineapple juice
30ml coconut cream
15ml Malibu
15ml sugar syrup (see page 4)
1 cup ice cubes

COMBINE ingredients in jug of a blender; blend on high speed until smooth. Pour into glass.

GLASS 400ml tulip-shaped
GARNISH two pineapple leaves and two straws

BANANA COLADA (B)

30ml Bacardi
30ml coconut cream
30ml sugar syrup (see page 4)
30ml fresh cream
120ml pineapple juice
½ banana
ice

POUR all ingredients into blender, blend, then pour into serving glass.

GLASS 300ml fancy
GARNISH banana, pineapple and mint leaves

piña colada

PRETTY WOMAN (L)

30ml peach liqueur
20ml vodka
80ml ruby red grapefruit juice
40ml cranberry juice
1 small lime, cut into quarters
1 cup ice

PLACE peach liqueur, vodka, juice and one lime quarter in shaker and shake vigorously.
STRAIN into glass over ice.

GLASS 285ml highball
GARNISH 3 wedges of lime

KELLY'S COMFORT (L)

30ml Southern Comfort
30ml Baileys
60ml milk
4 strawberries
15ml sugar syrup (see page 4)
ice

POUR all ingredients into blender, blend until smooth, then pour into serving glass.

GLASS 285ml highball
GARNISH strawberry

RAFFLES SINGAPORE SLING (G)

dash Angostura bitters
30ml gin
15ml Triple Sec
15ml Benedictine
15ml cherry brandy
15ml fresh lime juice
30ml pineapple juice
30ml fresh orange juice
ice

POUR all ingredients, one after the other, into serving glass filled with ice, stir gently with swizzle stick.

GLASS 285ml highball.
GARNISH orange slice and a cherry

LEFT pretty woman
RIGHT kelly's comfort

CHERISH (L)

8 fresh or canned cherries, stoned and halved
15ml cherry brandy
15ml Malibu
15ml Frangelico
15ml raspberry liqueur
30ml fresh cream
½ cup ice cubes

PLACE cherries in jug of a blender; blend on low speed until crushed.
COMBINE cherries with remaining ingredients in a cocktail shaker.
Shake vigorously then strain into chilled glass.

GLASS 150ml cocktail
GARNISH dark chocolate curls and a straw

BAILEYS CRUNCH (L)

2 Oreo biscuits
60ml Baileys
30ml dark crème de cacao
30ml chocolate liqueur
1 cup crushed ice

PULL biscuits apart, remove white filling; crush biscuits with rolling pin
or meat mallet.
COMBINE remaining ingredients in a cocktail shaker. Shake vigorously
then pour into chilled glass; sprinkle with crushed biscuits.

GLASS 150ml cocktail
GARNISH a straw

MUDSLIDE SHAKE (L)

20g chocolate, melted
1 cup crushed ice
30ml Baileys
30ml Kahlua
30ml vodka
30ml thickened cream
2 medium scoops vanilla ice-cream
1 medium scoop chocolate ice-cream

DRIZZLE melted chocolate around inside of glass; place glass upright in freezer for 5 minutes to set.

MEANWHILE, combine ice, Baileys, Kahlua, vodka and cream in jug of a blender; blend on high speed briefly. Add ice cream; blend on low speed until just combined, pour into glass.

GLASS 400ml fountain
GARNISH a straw

coconut mango thickshake

BANANA PASSIONFRUIT SOY SMOOTHIE (N)

You will need about six passionfruit for this recipe.

½ cup (125ml) passionfruit pulp
2 cups (500ml) soy milk
2 medium ripe bananas (400g), chopped coarsely

STRAIN passionfruit pulp through sieve into small bowl; reserve liquid and seeds.
BLEND passionfruit liquid, milk and banana, in batches, until smooth. Pour smoothie into large jug; stir in reserved seeds.

MAKES 1 litre (4 cups)

COCONUT MANGO THICKSHAKE (N)

3 medium mangoes (1.3kg)
200ml can coconut milk
1½ cups (375ml) milk
500ml vanilla ice-cream, chopped

CUT mango flesh from both sides of the seed. Remove the skin and freeze mango for several hours or until firm.
BLEND milks, mango and ice-cream, in two batches, until smooth. Serve immediately.

SERVES 6
TIPS For a reduced-fat version of the thickshake, substitute light coconut milk, skimmed milk and low-fat ice-cream. You can also use peaches, nectarines, plums, apricots, bananas or berries, or a combination if you prefer, instead of the mango.

banana passionfruit soy smoothie

MANGO FRAPPÉ (N)

2 medium mangoes (860g)
3 cups ice cubes
1 tablespoon sugar

HALVE mangoes, peel, then discard seeds. Blend or process mango flesh with ice cubes and sugar until thick and smooth.
POUR into serving glasses; stand at room temperature for 5 minutes before serving.

MAKES 3 cups (750ml)

FRESH BERRY FRAPPÉ (N)

300g blueberries
250g raspberries
4 cups crushed ice
1 cup (250ml) fresh orange juice

BLEND berries until just smooth. Push berry puree through fine sieve into large bowl; discard solids in sieve.
STIR in ice and juice and spoon into serving glasses; serve immediately.

MAKES 1 litre (4 cups)

fresh berry frappé

TIPS Depending on the sweetness of the berries, you may need to add sugar. You can crush the ice in a blender or food processor. You can also use frozen berries for this recipe. Experiment with other berries – strawberries, blackberries, boysenberries – and adjust combinations to your taste.

mango frappé

REGENCY FRUIT COCKTAIL (N)

3 medium strawberries
½ medium banana
2 x 5cm pieces pineapple
60ml fresh orange juice
60ml bottled pineapple juice
1 cup crushed ice

COMBINE ingredients in jug of a blender; blend on high speed until smooth, pour into glass.

GLASS 300ml highball
GARNISH a strawberry and a straw

RASPBERRY CRANBERRY CRUSH (N)

1 cup (250ml) raspberry sorbet
2 cups (500ml) cranberry juice
1 cup (150g) frozen raspberries
2 tablespoons lemon juice

BLEND or process ingredients until smooth. Serve immediately.

MAKES 1 litre (4 cups)
TIP Add a little icing sugar if you prefer this drink sweeter.

POM POM (N)

30ml fresh lemon juice
½ egg white
5ml grenadine
chilled lemonade
ice

POUR juice, egg white and grenadine into shaker, shake, then strain into serving glass. Top with lemonade and ice, pouring slowly.

GLASS 285ml highball
GARNISH lemon slice and cherry

raspberry cranberry crush

EUROPA'S VIRGINITY (N)

4 x 5cm pieces watermelon
½ cup crushed ice
60ml bottled apple juice
90ml lemonade

COMBINE watermelon and ice in jug of a blender; blend on high speed until smooth. Pour into glass; top up with apple juice and lemonade.

GLASS 300ml highball
GARNISH a straw

HOMEMADE LEMONADE (N)

4 medium lemons (560g)
4 cups (880g) caster sugar
2 cups (500ml) water
5 litres (20 cups) mineral water

REMOVE rind from lemons using a vegetable peeler, avoiding white pith; reserve lemons.
COMBINE rind, sugar and the water in large saucepan; stir over low heat, without boiling, until sugar is dissolved. Bring to a boil, simmer, uncovered, without stirring, about 10 minutes or until syrup is thickened slightly; cool.
SQUEEZE juice from lemons – you will need 1 cup (250ml) lemon juice. Add juice to syrup, strain into jug; cover, keep refrigerated.
JUST before serving, add four parts mineral water to one part lemonade, or to taste.

MAKES 6.25 litres (25 cups) diluted lemonade or 1.25 litres (5 cups) undiluted lemonade

homemade lemonade

SPICED TEA PUNCH (N)

1 litre (4 cups) water
4 teabags
1 cinnamon stick
2 cardamom pods
4 whole cloves
1 cup (220g) caster sugar
1½ cups (375ml) cold water, extra
½ cup (125ml) fresh lemon juice
2 cups (500ml) fresh orange juice
1 medium lemon (140g), sliced
¼ cup coarsely chopped fresh mint
1 litre (4 cups) mineral water
ice cubes

BRING the water to a boil in a large saucepan; add teabags, spices and sugar. Stir over low heat for about 3 minutes or until sugar is dissolved; discard teabags. Refrigerate until cold.
DISCARD spices then stir in the extra water, juices, lemon and mint. Just before serving, add mineral water and ice cubes.

MAKES 3 litres (12 cups)
TIP The tea mixture can be made a day ahead; store, covered, in the refrigerator.

MIXED BERRY PUNCH (N)

1 teabag
1 cup (250ml) boiling water
120g raspberries
150g blueberries
125g strawberries, halved
¼ cup loosely packed fresh
mint leaves
750ml chilled sparkling apple cider
2½ cups (625ml) chilled lemonade

PLACE teabag in heatproof mug, cover with the water; stand 10 minutes. Squeeze teabag over mug, discard teabag; cool tea 10 minutes. CRUSH raspberries in punch bowl with a fork; add blueberries, strawberries, mint and tea. Stir to combine, cover; refrigerate 1 hour. Stir cider and lemonade into punch just before serving; sprinkle with extra mint leaves, if desired.

SERVES 8

PRE-DINNER

NEGRONI (G)

For a longer, sweeter drink, omit the lemon rind from this recipe and top the drink up with 30ml soda water.

1 cup ice cubes
5cm piece lemon rind
45ml gin
30ml vermouth rosso
45ml Campari

PLACE ice and rind in glass; pour gin, vermouth and Campari over ice, one after the other.

GLASS 180ml old-fashioned
GARNISH a straw

GIN & IT (G)

30ml gin
30ml bianco vermouth
ice

POUR all ingredients into mixing glass filled with ice, stir, then strain into serving glass.

GLASS 90ml cocktail glass
GARNISH red cherry

PINK GIN (G)

dash Angostura bitters
45ml gin
30ml water (optional)

COAT inside of cocktail glass with bitters, add chilled gin then cold water if desired.

GLASS 90ml cocktail glass
GARNISH none

negroni

VANILLA MARTINI (V)

To make vanilla-infused vodka, combine 250ml vodka and 2 split vanilla beans in a glass jar, cover; stand for about 5 days or until the vodka is infused with vanilla flavour. Discard vanilla beans before using vodka.

45ml vanilla-infused vodka
10ml sugar syrup (see page 4)
15ml Frangelico
1 cup ice cubes

COMBINE ingredients in a cocktail shaker. Shake vigorously then strain into chilled glass.

GLASS 90ml martini

APPLE MARTINI (V)

45ml vodka
30ml apple schnapps
5ml sugar syrup (see page 4)
1 cup ice cubes

COMBINE ingredients in a cocktail shaker. Shake vigorously then strain into chilled glass.

GLASS 90ml martini
GARNISH sliver of green apple

vanilla martini

apple martini

dry martini

DRY MARTINI (G)

The best-known of the classic cocktails, the Martini seems simple in its composition yet there are endless subtle variations. The critical factor in a Martini is its dryness, so the amount of vermouth added is very important.

45ml gin
15ml dry vermouth
1 cup ice cubes

COMBINE ingredients in a cocktail shaker. Shake vigorously then strain into chilled glass.

GLASS 90ml martini
GARNISH a caperberry

GIMLET (G)

45ml gin
15ml lime juice cordial
ice

POUR all ingredients into mixing glass filled with ice, stir, then strain into serving glass.

GLASS 90ml cocktail glass
GARNISH lemon twist

CHAMPAGNE COCKTAIL (Ch)

1 sugar cube
6 drops Angostura bitters
15ml brandy or cognac
chilled champagne

SOAK sugar cube with bitters and drop into champagne flute, pour brandy or cognac on top of bitters, then fill with chilled champagne.

GLASS 140ml champagne flute
GARNISH orange slice

PLANTER'S PUNCH (B)

Bacardi or dark rum can be used, though the slightly darker rum has a stronger flavour.

1 cup ice cubes
50ml Bacardi
25ml fresh lime juice
20ml lime juice cordial
dash Angostura bitters
30ml soda water

COMBINE ice, Bacardi, juice, cordial and bitters in a cocktail shaker. Shake vigorously, then pour mixture into a glass; top with chilled soda water, stir.

GLASS 300ml highball
GARNISH a straw

FROZEN TEQUILA SUNRISE (T)

30ml tequila
90ml orange juice
concentrate, frozen
1½ cups ice cubes
10ml grenadine

COMBINE tequila, juice and ice in jug of a blender; blend until smooth, pour into glass.
CAREFULLY drizzle grenadine, over the back of a tablespoon, around inside rim of glass.

GLASS 300ml highball
GARNISH a straw

AMERICANO (C)

30ml Campari
30ml rosso vermouth
ice
soda water

POUR Campari then vermouth into serving glass filled with ice. Top with soda water, stir if desired.

GLASS 185ml old-fashioned
GARNISH lemon and lime wedges

POINSOTTA (L)

20ml Cointreau
40ml cranberry juice
sparkling wine or champagne

POUR Cointreau and juice into glass and top with sparkling wine or champagne.

GLASS 180ml champagne flute
GARNISH maraschino cherry

FRENCH 95 (Bb)

15ml bourbon
15ml fresh lemon juice
15ml sugar syrup (see page 4)
ice
chilled champagne

POUR bourbon, lemon juice and sugar syrup into shaker with ice, shake, then strain into serving glass. Top with champagne.

GLASS 140ml champagne flute
GARNISH lemon twist

LEFT americano
CENTRE poinsotta
RIGHT french 95

manhattan

MANHATTAN (W)

Another classic, and perhaps the best known of all the whisky cocktails. Rye and bourbon are preferred to scotch whisky in this recipe; sweet vermouth is believed to blend better with whiskies than dry.

60ml rye whisky
30ml vermouth rosso
1 cup ice cubes

COMBINE ingredients in a cocktail shaker. Shake vigorously then strain into a chilled glass.

GLASS 150ml margarita
GARNISH a maraschino cherry dropped in the glass

WHISKY SOUR (W)

45ml whisky
30ml fresh lemon juice
15ml sugar syrup (see page 4)
½ egg white (optional)

POUR all ingredients into shaker, shake, then strain into serving glass.

GLASS 180ml wine glass
GARNISH red cherry at bottom of glass, lemon slice on side of glass

SHERRY FLIP (S)

60ml cream sherry
1 egg
ice

POUR all ingredients into blender, blend until smooth, then pour into serving glass.

GLASS 140ml wine glass
GARNISH sprinkle of nutmeg

The Daiquiri was created in a small Cuban town of the same name by an American engineer, who combined the local spirit (rum) with native limes to make the ultimate pick-me up after a hot day in the iron mines.

traditional daiquiri

TRADITIONAL DAIQUIRI (B)

45ml Bacardi
30ml fresh lime juice
15ml sugar syrup (see page 4)
1 cup ice cubes

COMBINE ingredients in a cocktail shaker. Shake vigorously then strain into a glass.

GLASS 150ml cocktail

STRAWBERRY DAIQUIRI (B)

4 ripe strawberries
30ml Bacardi
30ml Cointreau
30ml lemon juice
ice

POUR all ingredients into blender, blend, then strain into serving glass.

GLASS 140ml champagne saucer
GARNISH strawberry

FROZEN MANGO DAIQUIRI (B)

To make this granita-like concoction, we recommend blending the ice with the mango for about 20 seconds, alternating between low and high speed, before adding the other ingredients. Don't make this drink too far in advance because it can become watery.

60ml Bacardi
60ml mango liqueur
30ml fresh lime juice
1 medium ripe mango, peeled, chopped coarsely
1 cup ice cubes

COMBINE ingredients in jug of a blender; blend until just combined, pour into glass.

GLASS 300ml highball

PASSIONFRUIT & PINEAPPLE DAIQUIRI (B)

We used canned passionfruit in syrup for this cocktail, which is available from supermarkets.

45ml Bacardi
30ml passionfruit in syrup
30ml bottled pineapple juice
15ml Cointreau
15ml fresh lime juice
1 cup ice cubes

COMBINE ingredients in a cocktail shaker. Shake vigorously then strain into a chilled glass.

GLASS 150ml cocktail
GARNISH a pineapple spear

MARGARITA (T)

You can use triple sec or white curaçao instead of Cointreau, if you prefer.

45ml tequila
30ml fresh lime juice
30ml Cointreau
1 cup ice cubes

COMBINE ingredients in a cocktail shaker. Shake vigorously then strain into a salt-rimmed (see page 5) glass.

GLASS 150ml margarita
GARNISH a slice of lemon

PINEAPPLE & MINT MARGARITA (T)

30ml tequila
15ml Cointreau
30ml fresh lime juice
30ml bottled pineapple juice
4 fresh mint leaves
1 cup ice cubes

COMBINE ingredients in jug of a blender; blend on high speed until well combined. Pour mixture into a salt-rimmed (see page 5) glass.

GLASS 150ml cocktail
GARNISH a small wedge of lemon and a sprig of mint

pineapple & mint margarita

CHILLI MARGARITA (T)

For a frozen chilli margarita, blend ingredients together in jug of a blender then pour into a cocktail glass.

20ml tequila
10ml Cointreau
45ml hot and sour mix
(see page 5)
dash Tabasco sauce
1 cup ice cubes

COMBINE ingredients in a cocktail shaker. Shake vigorously then strain into a glass.

GLASS 150ml margarita
GARNISH A slice of lime and a curled fresh red chilli

FROZEN STRAWBERRY MARGARITA (T)

30ml tequila
15ml Cointreau
15ml strawberry liqueur
30ml fresh lime juice
4 frozen strawberries
1 cup ice cubes

COMBINE ingredients in jug of a blender; blend until smooth.
Pour mixture into salt-rimmed (see page 5) glass.

GLASS 150ml margarita
GARNISH a strawberry wedge

IMPERIAL MARGARITA (T)

45ml tequila
30ml orange curaçao
30ml Cointreau
15ml fresh lime juice
1 cup ice cubes

COMBINE ingredients in
a cocktail shaker. Shake
vigorously then strain into a
salt-rimmed (see page 5) glass.

GLASS 150ml margarita

imperial margarita

87

iceberg

ICEBERG (L)

30ml Cointreau
30ml gin
¼ lime
sparkling wine
5 drops blue curaçao
1 cup ice

POUR Cointreau, gin and juice from lime into blender with ice and blend. Pour into chilled glass. Top with sparkling wine and drizzle blue curaçao on top.

GLASS 90/120ml martini glass
GARNISH 1 maraschino cherry

STINGER (Br)

45ml brandy
15ml white crème de menthe
ice

POUR all ingredients into mixing glass filled with ice, stir, then strain into serving glass.

GLASS 90ml cocktail glass
GARNISH none

SIDECAR (Br)

30ml brandy
30ml Cointreau
30ml fresh lemon juice
ice

POUR all ingredients into shaker, shake, then strain into serving glass.

GLASS 90ml cocktail glass
GARNISH lemon twist

GRENADINE RICKEY (N)

½ cup ice cubes
30ml grenadine
10ml fresh lime juice
180ml soda water

COMBINE ice, grenadine and lime juice in glass; top with soda, stir to blend.

GLASS 300ml highball
GARNISH a wedge of lime, a swizzle stick and a straw

LIME & MINT SPRITZER (N)

1 cup (250ml) lime juice
1.25 litres (5 cups) chilled mineral water
¼ cup coarsely chopped fresh mint
½ cup (125ml) sugar syrup (see page 4)

COMBINE syrup in large jug with juice, mineral water and mint. Serve immediately, with ice if desired.

SERVES 8

CINDERELLA (N)

60ml orange juice
60ml pineapple juice
60ml fresh lemon juice
ice

POUR all ingredients into shaker, shake, then pour into serving glass.

GLASS 285ml highball
GARNISH fruit in season

lime & mint spritzer

tomato, apple
& ginger punch

TROPICAL PUNCH (N)

You need half a medium pineapple, weighing approximately 650g, for this recipe.

425g can sliced mango in natural juice
3 cups (750ml) tropical fruit juice
300g finely chopped pineapple
250g finely chopped strawberries
2 tablespoons finely shredded fresh mint
1 tablespoon caster sugar
3 cups (750ml) dry ginger ale

STRAIN mango over small bowl; reserve juice. Chop mango slices finely; combine mango and reserved juice in large bowl with tropical fruit juice. Stir in pineapple, strawberries, mint, sugar and ginger ale. REFRIGERATE punch 2 hours before serving.

MAKES 2.5 litres (10 cups)

tropical punch

TOMATO, APPLE & GINGER PUNCH (N)

1 medium red apple (150g)
8cm piece fresh ginger (40g), grated finely
125g strawberries, quartered
2 cups (500ml) apple juice
1½ cups (375ml) tomato juice
3 cups (750ml) dry ginger ale

CORE and chop apple. Over small bowl, press ginger between two teaspoons to extract juice; discard pulp. Combine apple and straw-berries in large jug, add ginger juice and remaining juices; mix well. COVER, refrigerate until cold. Just before serving, add cold ginger ale.

MAKES 2 litres (8 cups)
TIP This recipe can be made a day ahead, but hold off on adding the ginger ale until just before serving.

PINEAPPLE ORANGE FRAPPÉ (N)

1 medium pineapple (1.25kg), chopped coarsely
½ cup (125ml) orange juice
3 cups crushed ice
1 tablespoon finely grated orange rind

BLEND pineapple and juice, in batches, until smooth.
POUR into large jug with crushed ice and rind; stir to combine.
Serve immediately.

MAKES 1 litre (4 cups)

SPARKLING FRUITY PUNCH (N)

2 litres (8 cups) orange and passionfruit juice drink
850ml can unsweetened pineapple juice
250g strawberries, chopped
¼ cup (60ml) passionfruit pulp
2 medium red apples (300g), chopped
2 medium oranges (360g), peeled, chopped
1.25 litres (5 cups) lemon soda squash
1.25 litres (5 cups) cream soda
3 cups (750ml) ginger beer
fresh mint sprigs

COMBINE orange and passionfruit juice drink, pineapple juice and fruit in large bowl.
STIR in remaining ingredients just before serving. Serve cold.

MAKES 6.5 litres (26 cups)
TIPS Refrigerate all ingredients before making the punch. Punch base can be prepared several hours ahead; add sparkling drinks just before serving.

sparkling fruity punch

AFTER DINNER

CHOCOLATE MARTINI (V)

10g chocolate, melted
1 cup ice cubes
45ml vodka
20ml white crème de cacao
45ml chocolate liqueur
10ml raspberry liqueur
20ml Baileys

USING melted chocoate, trace outline of a 9cm-circle (or the diameter of the glass rim) on a flat plate; twist the rim of glass in the choclate before it sets. Briefly place glass upright in freezer to set chocolate.
COMBINE half of the ice, vodka and crème de cacao in a cocktail shaker. Shake vigorously then strain into glass.
COMBINE remaining ice, liqueurs and Baileys in cocktail shaker. Shake vigorously then pour gently into glass over the back of a tablespoon so mixture floats. Do not stir.

GLASS 150ml cocktail
GARNISH grated chocolate and a raspberry

SILVER SUNSET (V)

30ml vodka
15ml Campari
15ml apricot brandy
90ml fresh orange juice
½ egg white
ice

POUR all ingredients into shaker, shake, then pour into serving glass.

GLASS 285ml highball
GARNISH orange slice and cherry

chocolate martini

BLACK RUSSIAN (V)

Tia Maria or dark crème de cacao can be substituted for Kahlua.

½ cup ice cubes
30ml vodka
30ml Kahlua
120ml cola, optional

PLACE ice in glass; pour vodka then Kahlua over ice.
Top with cola, if desired.

GLASS 180ml old-fashioned
GARNISH a straw

WHITE RUSSIAN (V)

½ cup ice cubes
30ml vodka
30ml Kahlua
30ml fresh cream

PLACE ice in glass; pour vodka then Kahlua over ice. Gently pour cream into glass over the back of a tablespoon so cream floats. Do not stir.

GLASS 180ml old-fashioned
GARNISH a straw

white russian

KIR ROYALE (L)

30ml crème de cassis
100ml chilled brut champagne

POUR crème de cassis into a chilled
flute; top with chilled champagne.

GLASS 150ml
CHAMPAGNE flute

kir royale

OLD-FASHIONED (W)

1 sugar cube
Angostura bitters
30ml soda water
ice
60ml scotch whisky
or bourbon

SOAK sugar cube with bitters and place into serving glass. Cover cube
with soda water, crush and mix to dissolve cube. Add ice, stir, then add
scotch whisky.

GLASS 180ml old-fashioned
GARNISH orange and lemon slices, and a cherry

PEACH MYRRH (L)

30ml peach liqueur
5ml vodka
40ml ruby red grapefruit juice
sparkling wine

POUR peach liqueur, vodka and juice into glass and top with sparkling wine.

GLASS 180ml champagne flute
GARNISH ½ strawberry or twist of lime

PERFECT LOVE (V)

30ml vodka
15ml Parfait Amour
15ml maraschino
ice

POUR ingredients, one after the other, into serving glass filled with ice.

GLASS 140ml old-fashioned
GARNISH lemon twist

EL BURRO (L)

15ml Kahlua
15ml dark rum
30ml cream of coconut
30ml fresh cream
½ banana
ice

POUR all ingredients into blender, blend until smooth, then pour into serving glass.

GLASS 180ml old-fashioned
GARNISH banana slice and mint leaves

peach myrrh

illusion

ILLUSION (L)

45ml Midori
20ml Cointreau
20ml vodka
60ml bottled pineapple juice
20ml fresh lime juice
1 cup ice cubes

COMBINE ingredients in a cocktail shaker. Shake vigorously then strain into a glass.

GLASS 240ml red wine
GARNISH thin slices of lime

YELLOW BIRD (B)

30ml Bacardi
22ml Galliano
22ml Cointreau
22ml fresh lime juice
ice

POUR all ingredients into shaker, shake, then pour into serving glass.

GLASS 180ml old-fashioned
GARNISH slice of lime in drink

BLACK VELVET (Be)

stout beer
champagne

POUR equal quantities of ingredients into serving glass. Stir if desired.

GLASS champagne flute

LEMONGRASS & GINGER ICED TEA (N)

6 lemongrass and ginger teabags
1 litre (4 cups) boiling water
2 tablespoons grated palm sugar
10cm stick fresh lemongrass (20g),
chopped finely
½ small orange (90g), sliced thinly
½ lemon, sliced thinly
¼ cup firmly packed fresh
mint leaves, torn
1 cup ice cubes

PLACE teabags and the water in large heatproof jug; stand 5 minutes.
DISCARD teabags. Add sugar, lemon grass, orange and lemon to jug;
stir to combine. Refrigerate, covered, until cold.
STIR mint into cold tea; serve immediately over ice.

MAKES 1 litre (4 cups)

SWEET SAFFRON LASSI (N)

*Lassis are yogurt-based drinks which are an excellent cooling foil for
a fiery Indian curry.*

pinch saffron threads
1 tablespoon boiling water
2 cups (560g) plain yogurt
1 cup (250ml) iced water
2 tablespoons caster sugar
½ teaspoon ground cardamom
ice cubes

COMBINE saffron and the boiling water in small heatproof cup; stand
5 minutes.
WHISK yogurt, the iced water, sugar and cardamom in large jug; stir in
saffron mixture.
SERVE lassi over ice cubes.

MAKES 3 cups (750ml)

NIGHTCAPS

BRANDY ALEXANDER (Br)

45ml brandy
30ml dark crème de cacao
60ml fresh cream
1 cup ice cubes

COMBINE ingredients in a cocktail shaker. Shake vigorously then strain into a glass.

GLASS 150ml cocktail
GARNISH cross two straws over the rim of glass; lightly sprinkle ground nutmeg over surface of drink, remove straws carefully

BETWEEN THE SHEETS (Br)

30ml brandy
30ml Bacardi
30ml Cointreau
7ml fresh lemon juice
ice

POUR all ingredients into shaker, shake, then strain into serving glass.

GLASS 140ml champagne saucer
GARNISH lemon twist

HOT TODDY (W)

60ml scotch whisky (or any preferred spirit or liqueur)
1 teaspoon honey or brown sugar
boiling water

POUR whisky into serving glass, add honey or sugar then top with boiling water.

GLASS 140ml wine glass
GARNISH lemon slice studded with cloves, a cinnamon stick and a sprinkle of nutmeg

brandy alexander

bounty

BOUNTY (L)

We used Monin coconut syrup for this cocktail, available from delicatessens and liquor shops.

30ml Baileys
15ml Kahlua
15ml coconut syrup
60ml fresh cream
1 cup ice cubes

COMBINE ingredients in jug of a blender; blend on high speed until well combined, pour into glass.

GLASS 180ml brandy balloon
GARNISH pineapple leaf and a straw

FLUFFY DUCK (B)

30ml Bacardi
30ml advocaat
ice
lemonade
cream

POUR Bacardi and advocaat into serving glass filled with ice and top with lemonade, mix well. Pour cream over a spoon so it overflows the spoon and floats on the surface of the drink.

GLASS 285ml highball
GARNISH strawberry

CASABLANCA (B)

30ml Bacardi
90ml pineapple juice
30ml coconut cream
15ml grenadine
ice

POUR all ingredients into blender, blend until smooth, then pour into a serving glass.

GLASS 285ml highball
GARNISH pineapple slices and a cherry

B52 (L)

30ml Kahlua
30ml Baileys
30ml Cointreau
ice

POUR ingredients, one after the other, into serving glass filled with ice and stir with swizzle stick.

GLASS 180ml old-fashioned

ATLANTIC PASSION (V)

We used canned passionfruit in syrup, available from supermarkets.
To make fresh strawberry juice, blend or process 250g fresh strawberries,
then push through a fine sieve. We rimmed the cocktail glass with pink
sugar; simply add a drop of red food colouring to sugar and mix well.

30ml vodka
60ml fresh strawberry puree
15ml passionfruit in syrup
10ml sugar syrup (see page 4)
1 cup ice cubes

COMBINE ingredients in a cocktail shaker. Shake vigorously then strain into chilled sugar-rimmed (see page 5) glass.

GLASS 150ml cocktail
GARNISH twist of orange rind

RUSTY NAIL (W)

45ml scotch whisky
22ml Drambuie
ice

POUR the ingredients, one on top of the other, over ice in serving glass.

GLASS 180ml old-fashioned
GARNISH lemon twist

SARAH JANE (B)

30ml Bacardi
15ml Grand Marnier
15ml apricot brandy
30ml orange juice
30ml fresh cream
7ml Galliano
ice

POUR all ingredients into shaker, shake, then strain into serving glass.

GLASS 140ml champagne saucer
GARNISH chocolate flake, a strawberry

atlantic passion

flirtini

FLIRTINI (V)

6 fresh raspberries
1 cup ice cubes
30ml vodka
15ml Cointreau
15ml cranberry juice
15ml fresh lime juice
15ml bottled pineapple juice
60ml brut champagne

CRUSH raspberries in base of chilled glass; top with half of the ice.
COMBINE remaining ice, vodka, Cointreau and juices in a cocktail shaker.
Shake vigorously then strain into glass; top with champagne.

GLASS 300ml highball
GARNISH extra fresh raspberries threaded onto a toothpick and balanced across rim of glass

GLÜHWEIN (Wi)

1 bottle red wine
3 tablespoons sugar
2 slices lemon
2 slices orange
1 cinnamon stick

WARM all ingredients in a saucepan until very hot. Do not boil. Serve in a heated glass.

GLASS 140ml wine glass

HOT BUTTERED RUM (R)

1 small slice butter
1 teaspoon brown sugar
cinnamon
nutmeg
vanilla extract
30ml dark rum
boiling water

MIX butter, brown sugar, cinnamon, nutmeg and vanilla until creamed.
Place one teaspoon into a serving glass, pour dark rum and boiling water into serving glass and mix well.

GLASS 180ml stemmed wine glass

REAL HOT CHOCOLATE (L)

1 litre (4 cups) milk
200g milk eating chocolate, chopped
100g dark eating chocolate, chopped
¾ cup (180ml) whipping cream
1 tablespoon Tia Maria or Baileys
90g Maltesers, chopped

COMBINE milk and both chocolates in medium saucepan; stir over low heat until chocolate is melted. Do not boil milk.
BEAT cream and liqueur in small bowl of electric mixer until soft peaks form.
DIVIDE milk among heatproof serving glasses, top with cream mixture and sprinkle with chopped Maltesers.

SERVES 6

EGGNOG (Br)

5ml sugar syrup (see page 4)
30ml brandy
30ml dark rum
1 egg
ice
90ml milk

POUR sugar syrup, brandy, rum, egg and ice into blender, blend, pour into serving glass then top up with milk. Stir.

GLASS 285ml highball
GARNISH nutmeg and a cherry
TIP for hot eggnog, omit ice and add hot milk

real hot chocolate

GLOSSARY

ADVOCAAT A Dutch liqueur made from egg yolks, sugar and brandy.

AMARETTO an Italian liqueur made from apricot seeds with a decided almond flavour.

ANGOSTURA BITTERS the best-known brand of bitters; an aromatic essence of herbs, roots and bark.

APPLE SCHNAPPS an apple-flavoured version of the clear German spirit distilled from various grains or potatoes.

BACARDI brand name of the original Cuban rum. We used Bacardi Carta Blanca, a clear refined rum aged in white oak.

BAILEYS a liqueur made from cream, Irish whiskey and spirits.

BOURBON authentic American whiskey originating in Bourbon County, Kentucky; it's made from at least 51% corn, and aged in charred oak for a minimum two years.

BRANDY a liqueur made from distilled fermented grapes. If made from any other fruit, the fruit type is included in the name, e.g., apple brandy.

CAMPARI Italian brand of bitters; deep-red in colour with a bittersweet orange taste.

CHAMPAGNE a light sparkling wine, made in France by the *méthode champenoise*. Labels indicate level of sweetness: brut is the driest; extra-dry is less dry; sec is sweet; and demi-sec is even sweeter.

CHERRY BRANDY A liqueur made from the juice of cherries and brandy.

COCONUT CREAM first pressing from grated coconut flesh; available in cans and cartons.

COCONUT MILK not the juice found inside the fruit, which is known as coconut water, but the diluted liquid from the second pressing of the white flesh of a mature coconut (the first pressing produces coconut cream). Available in cans and cartons at supermarkets.

COCONUT SYRUP a mixture of sugar, water and artificial or natural coconut flavouring; we used Monin coconut syrup in this book, available from supermarkets and off-licences.

COGNAC Brandy from the Cognac region in France.

COINTREAU a French liqueur; clear orange-flavoured brandy.

CREAM fresh: (minimum fat content 35%) also known as pure cream and pouring cream; has no additives like commercially thickened cream; whipping: (minimum fat content 35%) a thickened cream containing a thickener.

CREAM SODA a sweet carbonated drink.

CRÈME DE CACAO a liqueur made from cocoa beans and vanilla. It comes in two colours, dark and white (clear).

CRÈME DE CASSIS a liqueur made from blackcurrants.

CRÈME DE MENTHE A pepper-mint-flavoured liqueur which is available in white, green and red.

CURAÇAO named after the Caribbean island where the oranges for the original blend of this liqueur were grown. The most common colour is white (clear), but there are also orange, red, green and blue versions.

DRAMBUIE A liqueur based on Scotch and heather honey.

FRANGELICO an Italian hazelnut-flavoured liqueur.

GALLIANO A gold-coloured liqueur with a licorice and aniseed flavour.

GIN an un-aged clear spirit distilled from grain alcohol, juniper berries and herbs.

KEY TO SYMBOLS

To help you choose your perfect cocktail, we have provided a symbol next to the title giving the base alcohol used in each recipe.

(B)   Bacardi

(Bb)   Bourbon

(Be)   Beer

(Br)   Brandy

(C)   Campari

(Ch)   Champagne

(G)   Gin

(L)   Liqueur

(N)   Non-alcoholic

(R)   Rum

(S)   Sherry

(T)   Tequila

(V)   Vodka

(W)   Whisky

(Wi)   Wine

GINGER ALE a ginger-flavoured carbonated drink.

GINGER BEER available in both non-alcoholic and alcoholic versions; made of ginger, sugar, water and yeast.

GRAND MARNIER A golden-brown French brandy liqueur with an orange flavour.

GRENADINE originally made from pomegranates grown on Caribbean island, Grenada; a dark-red non-alcoholic sugar syrup used to colour and sweeten cocktails and desserts.

KAHLUA a brandy-based liqueur flavoured with coffee.

LEMON SODA SQUASH a lemon-flavoured carbonated drink.

LEMON SORBET also known as sherbet or granita.

LEMONGRASS a tall, clumping, lemon-smelling and tasting, sharp-edged grass; the white lower part of the stem is used, finely chopped, in cooking.

LIMONCELLO Italian lemon-flavoured liqueur.

MALIBU brand name of a rum-based coconut liqueur.

MALTESERS chocolates with crisp, light honeycomb centres.

MARASCHINO A colourless Italian cherry-flavoured liqueur.

MIDORI green Japanese liqueur made from honeydew melon.

OREO BISCUITS brand name of an American 'cookie'; two small round chocolate biscuits enclosing a creme filling.

PALM SUGAR a dark brown to black sugar from the coconut palm, sold in cakes; also known as gula jawa, gula melaka and jaggery.

PARFAIT AMOUR A perfumed French liqueur made from lemons, oranges, brandy and herbs; light purple in colour.

PERNOD A French aperitif. Pernod 45 has an aniseed flavour; Pernod Pastis has a licorice flavour.

RUM a distillation of fermented sugar cane; colour varies from white (clear) to dark.

SAFFRON stigma of a member of the crocus family, available in strands or ground form; imparts a yellow-orange colour to food once infused. Quality varies greatly; the best is the most expensive spice in the world. Should be stored in the freezer.

SCOTCH WHISKY made in Scotland from a distillation of malted or unmalted barley dried with peat smoke and matured in oak at least three years.

SOUTHERN COMFORT An American liqueur with a brandy and bourbon base and a peach flavour.

TABASCO SAUCE brand name of a fiery sauce made from vinegar, red peppers and salt.

TEQUILA made from mixture of fresh and fermented agave juice (pulque); double-distilled to produce white (clear) tequila. Gold tequila is aged in oak casks for up to four years.

TIA MARIA A Jamaican liqueur based on rum; has a coffee flavour.

TODDY A mixture of spirit and hot water.

TRIPLE SEC strong, white (clear), orange-flavoured liqueur similar to curaçao.

VERMOUTH a herb-flavoured fortified white wine available dry (white) and sweet (bianco or rosso).

VODKA an un-aged clear spirit distilled from grains such as barley, wheat or rye; also available in various citrus flavours.

WINE Usually the fermented juice of grapes.

WHISKY A distillation of grain, malt, sugar and yeast. Also Irish whiskey and rye whiskey.

WORCESTERSHIRE SAUCE thin, dark-brown spicy sauce used as a flavouring.

CONVERSION CHARTS

Measures

The cup and spoon measurements used in this book are metric: one measuring cup holds approximately 250ml; one metric tablespoon holds 20ml; one metric teaspoon holds 5ml.

All cup and spoon measurements are level. The most accurate way of measuring dry ingredients is to weigh them. When measuring liquids, use a clear glass or plastic jug with metric markings. We used large eggs with an average weight of 60g.

WARNING This book contains recipes for dishes made with raw or lightly cooked eggs. These should be avoided by vulnerable people such as pregnant and nursing mothers, invalids, the elderly, babies and young children.

Dry measures

metric	imperial
15g	½oz
30g	1oz
60g	2oz
90g	3oz
125g	4oz (¼lb)
155g	5oz
185g	6oz
220g	7oz
250g	8oz (½lb)
280g	9oz
315g	10oz
345g	11oz
375g	12oz (¾lb)
410g	13oz
440g	14oz
470g	15oz
500g	16oz (1lb)
750g	24oz (1½lb)
1kg	32oz (2lb)

Liquid measures

metric	imperial
30ml	1 fl oz
60ml	2 fl oz
100ml	3 fl oz
125ml	4 fl oz
150ml	5 fl oz (¼ pint/1 gill)
190ml	6 fl oz
250ml	8 fl oz
300ml	10 fl oz (½pt)
500ml	16 fl oz
600ml	20 fl oz (1 pint)
1000ml (1 litre)	1¾pints

Length measures

metric	imperial
3mm	⅛in
6mm	¼in
1cm	½in
2cm	¾in
2.5cm	1in
5cm	2in
6cm	2½in
8cm	3in
10cm	4in
13cm	5in
15cm	6in
18cm	7in
20cm	8in
23cm	9in
25cm	10in
28cm	11in
30cm	12in (1ft)

Oven temperatures

These oven temperatures are only a guide for conventional ovens. For fan-assisted ovens, check the manufacturer's manual.

	°C (Celcius)	°F (Fahrenheit)	gas mark
Very low	120	250	½
Low	150	275-300	1-2
Moderately low	170	325	3
Moderate	180	350-375	4-5
Moderately hot	200	400	6
Hot	220	425-450	7-8
Very hot	240	475	9

INDEX

ARE YOU MISSING SOME COOKBOOKS?

CANCELLED

The Australian Women's Weekly Cookbooks are available from bookshops, cookshops, supermarkets and other stores all over the world. You can also buy direct from the publisher, using the order form below.

TITLE	RRP	QTY	TITLE	RRP	QTY
100 Fast Fillets	£6.99		Grills	£6.99	
A Taste of Chocolate	£6.99		Indian Cooking Class	£6.99	
After Work Fast	£6.99		Japanese Cooking Class	£6.99	
Beginners Cooking Class	£6.99		Just For One	£6.99	
Beginners Thai	£6.99		Just For Two	£6.99	
Best Food Fast	£6.99		Kids' Birthday Cakes	£6.99	
Breads & Muffins	£6.99		Kids Cooking	£6.99	
Brunches, Lunches & Treats	£6.99		Kids' Cooking Step-by-Step	£6.99	
Cafe Classics	£6.99		Low-carb, Low-fat	£6.99	
Cafe Favourites	£6.99		Low-fat Food for Life	£6.99	
Cakes Bakes & Desserts	£6.99		Low-fat Meals in Minutes	£6.99	
Cakes Biscuits & Slices	£6.99		Main Course Salads	£6.99	
Cakes Cooking Class	£6.99		Mexican	£6.99	
Caribbean Cooking	£6.99		Middle Eastern Cooking Class	£6.99	
Casseroles	£6.99		Mince in Minutes	£6.99	
Casseroles & Slow-Cooked Classics	£6.99		Moroccan & the Foods of North Africa	£6.99	
Cheap Eats	£6.99		Muffins, Scones & Breads	£6.99	
Cheesecakes: baked and chilled	£6.99		New Casseroles	£6.99	
Chicken	£6.99		New Curries	£6.99	
Chicken Meals in Minutes	£6.99		New Finger Food	£6.99	
Chinese and the foods of Thailand, Vietnam, Malaysia & Japan	£6.99		New French Food	£6.99	
			New Salads	£6.99	
Chinese Cooking Class	£6.99		Party Food and Drink	£6.99	
Christmas Cooking	£6.99		Pasta Meals in Minutes	£6.99	
Chocs & Treats	£6.99		Potatoes	£6.99	
Cocktails	£6.99		Quick & Simple Cooking (Apr 08)	£6.99	
Cookies & Biscuits	£6.99		Rice & Risotto	£6.99	
Cooking Class Cake Decorating	£6.99		Sauces Salsas & Dressings	£6.99	
Cupcakes & Fairycakes	£6.99		Sensational Stir-Fries	£6.99	
Detox	£6.99		Simple Healthy Meals	£6.99	
Dinner Lamb	£6.99		Simple Starters Mains & Puds	£6.99	
Easy Comfort Food (May 08)	£6.99		Soup	£6.99	
Easy Curry	£6.99		Stir-fry	£6.99	
Easy Midweek Meals	£6.99		Superfoods for Exam Success	£6.99	
Easy Spanish-Style	£6.99		Tapas Mezze Antipasto & other bites	£6.99	
Food for Fit and Healthy Kids	£6.99		Thai Cooking Class	£6.99	
Foods of the Mediterranean	£6.99		Traditional Italian	£6.99	
Foods That Fight Back	£6.99		Vegetarian Meals in Minutes	£6.99	
Fresh Food Fast	£6.99		Vegie Food	£6.99	
Fresh Food for Babies & Toddlers	£6.99		Wicked Sweet Indulgences	£6.99	
Good Food for Babies & Toddlers	£6.99		Wok Meals in Minutes	£6.99	
Great Kids' Cakes (May 08)	£6.99				
Greek Cooking Class	£6.99		TOTAL COST:	£	

Mr/Mrs/Ms _____

Address _____

_____ Postcode _____

Day time phone _____ Email* (optional) _____

I enclose my cheque/money order for £ _____

or please charge £ _____

to my: ☐ Access   ☐ Mastercard   ☐ Visa   ☐ Diners Club

Card number ☐☐☐☐ ☐☐☐☐ ☐☐☐☐ ☐☐☐☐

Expiry date _____ 3 digit security code *(found on reverse of card)* _____

Cardholder's name_____ Signature _____

* By including your email address, you consent to receipt of any email regarding this magazine, and other emails which inform you of ACP's other publications, products, services and events, and to promote third party goods and services you may be interested in.

ACP BOOKS

General manager Christine Whiston
Test kitchen food director Pamela Clark
Editorial director Susan Tomnay
Creative director Hieu Chi Nguyen
Director of sales Brian Cearnes
Marketing manager Bridget Cody
Business analyst Rebecca Varela
Operations manager David Scotto
International rights enquiries Laura Bamford
lbamford@acpuk.com

ACP Books are published by ACP Magazines
a division of PBL Media Pty Limited

Group publisher, Women's lifestyle
Pat Ingram
Director of sales, Women's lifestyle
Lynette Phillips
Commercial manager, Women's lifestyle
Seymour Cohen
Marketing director, Women's lifestyle
Matthew Dominello
Public relations manager, Women's lifestyle
Hannah Deveraux
Creative director, Events, Women's lifestyle
Luke Bonnano
Research Director, Women's lifestyle
Justin Stone
ACP Magazines, Chief Executive officer
Scott Lorson
PBL Media, Chief Executive officer
Ian Law

Produced by ACP Books, Sydney.
Published by ACP Books, a division of
ACP Magazines Ltd, 54 Park St, Sydney;
GPO Box 4088, Sydney, NSW 2001.
phone (02) 9282 8618 fax (02) 9267 9438.
acpbooks@acpmagazines.com.au
www.acpbooks.com.au
Printed and bound in China.

Australia Distributed by Network Services,
phone +61 2 9282 8777 fax +61 2 9264 3278
networkweb@networkservicescompany.com.au
United Kingdom Distributed by Australian
Consolidated Press (UK),
phone (01604) 642 200 fax (01604) 642 300
books@acpuk.com
New Zealand Distributed by Netlink
Distribution Company,
phone (9) 366 9966 ask@ndc.co.nz
South Africa Distributed by PSD Promotions,
phone (27 11) 392 6065/6/7
fax (27 11) 392 6079/80
orders@psdprom.co.za
Canada Distributed by Publishers Group Canada
phone (800) 663 5714 fax (800) 565 3770
service@raincoast.com

A catalogue record for this book is available from
the British Library.
ISBN 978-1-903777-24-4
© ACP Magazines Ltd 2008
ABN 18 053 273 546
This publication is copyright. No part of it may be
reproduced or transmitted in any form without the written
permission of the publishers.